Theresa Lund Weber

POMPEII HERCULANEUM AND VESUVIUS

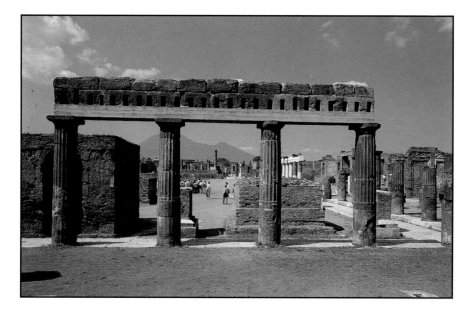

New Edition

BONECHI EDIZIONI "IL TURISMO" FIRENZE

Exclusive distributor for Napoli and Campania:
VERBEL & C. S.a.s.
di Mariarosaria Bello
Via Domenico Quaranta, 23
80126 NAPOLI (Loggetta)
Tel.-Fax (081) 59.39.446

VESUVIUS

Vesuvius' dark cone silhouetted against a bright blue Mediterranean sky is undoubtedly the most striking sight in the Gulf of Naples. Over 4000 feet tall, the volcano is composed of lava spit forth in the course of *eruptions of various intensity and duration (seventy-odd since the famous one that buried Pompeii and Herculaneum). Still active, it actually comprises two parts: an external crater, Monte Somma, and Vesuvius* *proper, which peaks in the so-called Gran Cono (Great Cone), the site of volcano activity.*

Up to the historic eruption of August 24, 79 A.D. Vesuvius' sole claim to fame was its excellent wine (known as Vesuvinum).

Preceding page: The Gran Cono.
Left: the bleak landscape on the
slopes of Vesuvius surrounding
the cone; *below*: an impressive
view inside the crater.

Thereafter, its name was associated with the death and destruction it left in its wake. In all fairness, however, the volcano should not be considered only a destructive force since the ash it periodically erupts contains high percentages of soil-enriching potassium, calcium, and sodium.

Today, it is possible to enjoy a splendid panorama from the summit while observing ominous fumarole smoke wisps that bring to mind the terrible events of the year 79. An eyewitness account has come down to us:

Pliny the Younger described the eruption and its effects on the victims (including the death of his uncle, the renowned naturalist, Pliny the Elder) in two letters written to their contemporary, the historian Tacitus. His words, better than any others, render the full horror of the fateful happening:

"A cloud began to gather – people watching from afar were unable to tell from whence it came, only later learning of Vesuvius. At first, it rose up like a gigantic treetrunk, thereafter splitting into a myriad of branches. I believe this happened because the cloud originated from an airstream, branching out only when the air stopped blowing or when the cloud became too heavy for its own weight. Its color varied,

Above: the mouth of the crater;
below: the volcano seen from the sea.

from time to time white, then dirt-colored and spotty from the soil and ashes it was carrying.

Pliny the Elder set out on a rowboat to bring comfort to the stricken, who were numerous due to the fact that the area was thickly populated. He headed to where everyone else was gathered in the midst of the danger zone. He was dauntless, so fearless as to be able to dictate descriptions of the phenomena as he witnessed them: the terrible happenings of that terrible day.

Ashes, hotter and denser the nearer one approached, spilled over the crater. Pomice and blackened stones, baked and molded by the fire, appeared, followed by an unexpected low-lying area and the shore obstructed by rocks spewed from the mountain. Pliny reached Stabia where Vesuvius looked as if it were spitting tongues of fire, rendered even brighter by the darkness of the night. My uncle did his best to calm the frightened survivors by telling them that the flames were issuing from farmbuildings abandoned by peasants as they fed the countryside. Then, he went back to get a good night's sleep. But the level of the courtyard through which one had to pass to reach his apartment was in the meantime rising so rapidly as ash and lapilli piled higher and higher that, had he remained any longer, he never would have managed to get out. Awakened, he fled to reach

Pomponian and the others who had not slept a wink the whole night. They discussed whether is was better to remain under the protection of a roof or else risk going out. Continuous and prolonged trembling of the earth caused the building to shake – jerking up and down, the walls gave the sensation of being detached from their very foundations. On the other hand, venturing outside meant braving the shower of lapilli, however lightweight and porous it appeared to be.

Nevertheless, he decided it would be wiser to risk being out in the open. In him, reason was the dominating force; in his companions, fear. To protect themselves, they tied cushions over their heads with torn sheets for straps.

Even though dawn had already broken, darkness, blacker than the darkest night, reigned everywhere, punctuated here and there by fires and other glares. He wanted to reach the beach so that he could decide from close up whether he would be able to set sail – but the sea was so choppy he could tell it would be impossible. So he lay down to rest upon a sheet spread out on the shore, after having drunk thirstily from his supply of drinking water. But finally the flames and smell of sulfur – warning of more flames to come – awakened him as they had so many before. He made an attempt to get to his feet aided by two slaves, but

immediately collapsed owing, I am sure, to the ash-infested air that had stifled his breathing by blocking his delicate and extremely narrow bronchial tubes which had always been a source of trouble to him.

When the day – the third after the one he had last seen complete – broke anew, his corpse was discovered intact and unharmed, still clothed; he looked as if he were sleeping rather than dead." (Epistles, Book VI.)

Pompeii and Stabia were buried beneath a mantle of ashes and lapilli in the course of the eruption, Herculaneum under a slew of mud in its aftermath. The toll in human lives was enormous: an estimated two thousand perished in Pompeii alone. The reigning Roman emperor, Titus, set up a rescue committee and ordered that all recovered objects be returned to their rightful owners.

The initial attempts at reconstructing Pompeii and the other stricken centers were rendered vain by new explosions, the eruptions of 202 and 472. In 512, Theodoric, king of the Goths, exempted the populace, ruined in still another eruption, from paying taxes. History records several other outbursts until the year 1139, after which for virtually five centuries the volcano failed to erupt even a single time. Then, on December 16, 1631, disaster struck once more: the eruption left three thousand dead and ruined farm– and pas-

turelands in its wake – with smoke blacking out the sky down to the Gulf of Taranto for several days. Thereafter, eruption followed eruption. Among the most terrible were those of 1694, 1767, 1794 (which razed the town of Torre del Greco to the ground), and 1906. Volcanic activity continued in our century, especially between 1933 and 1944 when Vesuvius could be seen with a great plume of smoke rising out of its crater. The last recorded eruption took place on March 31, 1944.

POMPEII

Pompeii is located south of Vesuvius in a splendid setting whose praises were sung by such great Latin authors as Seneca. It rises along a volcano-formed plateau about a hundred feet above sea level which, however, is wholly lacking in waterways or water sources. For this reason the earliest settlements in the nearby Sarno Valley do not date back later than the 8th century B.C. Pompeii itself was not settled until the mid 7th century - and most likely as little more than a station marking the intersection of the region's three major roadways, i.e., the carriage routes of Cuma, Nola, and Stabia.

Although Pompeii's earliest inhabitants belonged to an Italic people, the Osci, the name of their city is probably of Greek origin. Whatever the derivation, the city prospered, mainly on account of its favorable position along the coast which allowed it to compete with the Greek coastal cities, foremost of which Cuma, as the region's principal port. The Roman historian Strabo reports that Pompeii ranked as the main port for cities such as Nola, Acerrae, and Nuceria.

Nevertheless, it was impossible for the city to avoid falling under the influence of the all-powerful Greeks, whose domains in the Gulf of Naples encompassed the Sorrentine Peninsula and the Isles of Ischia and Capri. In the 6th century, however, a new threat arrived from the north: the Etruscans, after having conquered Latium, set out to subjugate Campania. Actually, their intention was to drive the Greeks, ensconced along the coast, right into the sea. Strabo's report on the Etruscan conquest of Pompeii has been corroborated by recent archeological finds, e.g. the numerous bucchero fragments with Etruscan inscriptions unearthed in the vicinity of the Temple of Apollo by the Stabian Baths, and, in the 6th century B.C. necropolis which came to light nearby.

The dominance of the Etruscans was shortlived. Defeated by the Cumeans and Siracusans in a great sea battle fought in the territorial waters of the city of Cuma in the mid 5th century B.C., they relinquished control of the coastal region which thus returned under Greek rule.

Shortly after the defeat of the Etruscans, the Samnites began to move from the mountains down toward the coastal zones, thereby initiating a slow but inexorable conquest of the region. (It took them the whole century, but they managed to conquer all of Campania, with the exception of Neapolis, i.e., present-day Naples)

The city of Pompeii underwent considerable transformation during the Samnite period, although existing architectural remains reveal predominant Greek rather than local influxes. Perhaps the most impressive project dating from this period was the great tufa fortification wall that encircled the whole plateau (150 acres) and not just the actual territory of the city (which at the time covered barely 25 acres).

In the 4th century B.C., Pompeii took part in a war waged by the Romans against the Samnites, which resulted in Rome's subjugation of the entire Campania region. Forced to accept the status of socia of the Urbs, the city nonetheless was able to preserve a certain amount of linguistic and governmental autonomy. Building activity was intense throughout this period: a town plan was drawn up and new city walls were built of Sarno limestone.

Unlike the majority of Campania cities, Pompeii remained loyal to Rome during the 3rd century B.C. when the Second

11

Punic War was fought. Such fidelity did not go unrewarded: the city was allowed to preserve her independence, albeit only in certain respects.

The 2nd century B.C. was Pompeii's period of glory. It grew and prospered as a folcrum of trade and commerce and as a great agricultural center (two of its major crops, grapes and olives, being exported all over Italy and abroad as wine and oil). The wealth of the city was reflected in the luxuriousness of Pompeian residences such as the House of the Faun whose ten thousand square feet could rival even the most grandiose of the Hellenistic mansions.

When the Social War broke out in 91 B.C., Pompeii, along with the other Campania cities, sided with those attempting to overthrow the status quo, and

The Dancing Faun in the Museo Archeologico Nazionale of Naples, originally from the House of the Faun.

Alexander the Great and Darius at the Battle of Issus, the magnificent floor mosaic of the exedra, from the House of the Faun, now in the Museo Archeologico Nazionale of Naples.

thereby attain full Roman citizenship. However, Rome was militarily superior to the upstarts who were speedily dealt with. Soon after, in 89 B.C., Silla set out first to crush Stabia and, when that was accomplished, to subdue Pompeii. The Pompeians put up a valient fight — after having farsightedly reinforced their city walls — under the leadership of a Celt, L. Cluentius. All efforts proved vain, however, and the city fell in 80 B.C., never again to exist outside the Roman sphere of influence. As was Roman practice, Silla divided up good chunks of Pom-

peian territory among his veterans who called their settlement Colonia Cornelia Veneria Pompeianorum. Despite the fact that this naturally created some conflicts with the local populace, business soon resumed as usual and, especially in the wine trade, markets increased in both number and distance. The city's year-round pleasant climate and lovely setting also attracted wealthy Romans, some of whom, like Cicero, bought property in the area, so that it soon became a popular vacation spot.

Unfortunately, very little regarding life in the Imperial Age

Below: reconstruction of the great eruption.
Opposite page: mosaics of a satyr and maenad (*top*); strolling musicians signed by Dioscuride of Samos (*center*); sea creatures (*bottom*).

CUMAE   CAPUA   ACERRA   fiume Sarno   SARNO   NUCER.

BAIA PUTEOLI   PARTENOPE   ERCOLANO   POMPEI   STABIAE
MISENO   NEAPOLIS   OPLONTO   Saline   Pago marittimo   SORRENTUM

(1st century B.C.) has survived. Tacitus informs us that, due to a brawl which broke out between the citizens of Nuceria and Pompeii in the Pompeii Amphitheater, the Roman emperor Nero banned gladiator sports in the arena for ten years.

The 1st century of the Christian Era brought not one, but two, tragedies to Pompeii. In the year 62 a terrible earthquake wrecked havoc on the whole Campania region, practically destroying Pompeii, Herculaneum, and numerous other inhabited areas in one fell swoop. When Vesuvius erupted the morning of August 24 in the year 79, reconstruction was far from being completed.

By the time the sun rose on that fateful morning, a great pine-shaped cloud could be seen billowing out of the crater. At ten o'clock, the first explosions could be heard: the gas imprisoned inside the crater burst through the solidified lava making up the peak and blew it to smithereens that poured over Pompeii as a shower of molten lapilli. The lapilli and ash blanket was so thick that even the sunlight was blocked out. What the lava, lapilli, and earthquakes left undone was finished by the poisonous gases — and no one was left to tell the tale. Two thousand people — out of a total estimated population of ten thousand — were poisoned, asphyxiated, or else crushed under the weight of toppling buildings.

Pompeii, buried under more than twenty feet of volcanic ash and debris, was forgotten for fifteen centuries. Then, in the late 1500s, several inscriptions– and even sone buildings–came to light during the digging of a canal off the Sarno. Nevertheless, the architect who made the discovery, Domenico Fontana, never realized that he had stumbled on the remains of historic Pompeii and failed to pursue his investigation.

The first real excavations were undertaken in 1748 under the patronage of King Carlo of Bourbon — although admittedly they were neither systematic nor scientific. Also, the early archeologists regrettably followed the then common practice of unearthing a building, despoiling it, and then burying it over once more. Excavations, however, continued throughout the 19th century, during which time practically the whole Forum and numerous residences were brought to light. When the Italian regions were united as a single kingdom in the 1860s, Giuseppe Fiorelli, appointed director of the digs, continued the project according to a more scientific approach. He was also able to devise a method for making plaster casts of the victims (i.e., liquid plaster poured into the spaces once occupied by the bodies around which volcanic ash had, in the course of two millennia, solidified), which better than words express the horror of their dying.

Plan of Pompeii

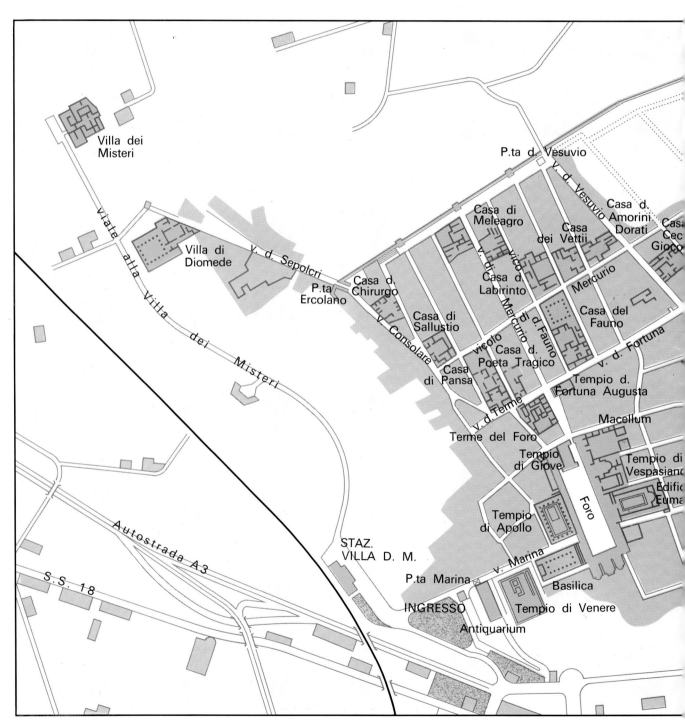

Villa dei Misteri

P.ta d. Vesuvio

V. d. Vesuvio

Casa d. Amorini Dorati

Casa Cec Gioco

Casa di Meleagro

Casa dei Vettii

V. di

Vicolo

Mercurio

Villa di Diomede

V. d. Sepolcri

Casa d. Labirinto

Mercurio

di d. Fauno

Casa del Fauno

V. d. Fortuna

P.ta Ercolano

Casa d. Chirurgo

Casa di Sallustio

vicolo

Casa d. Poeta Tragico

V. Consolare

Casa di Pansa

Tempio d. Fortuna Augusta

v. d. Terme

Macellum

Terme del Foro

Tempio di Giove

Tempio di Vespasiano

Edific Euma

Foro

Tempio di Apollo

STAZ. VILLA D. M.

v. Marina

Autostrada A3

P.ta Marina

S.S. 18

INGRESSO

Antiquarium

Basilica

Tempio di Venere

viale

alla

Villa

dei

Misteri

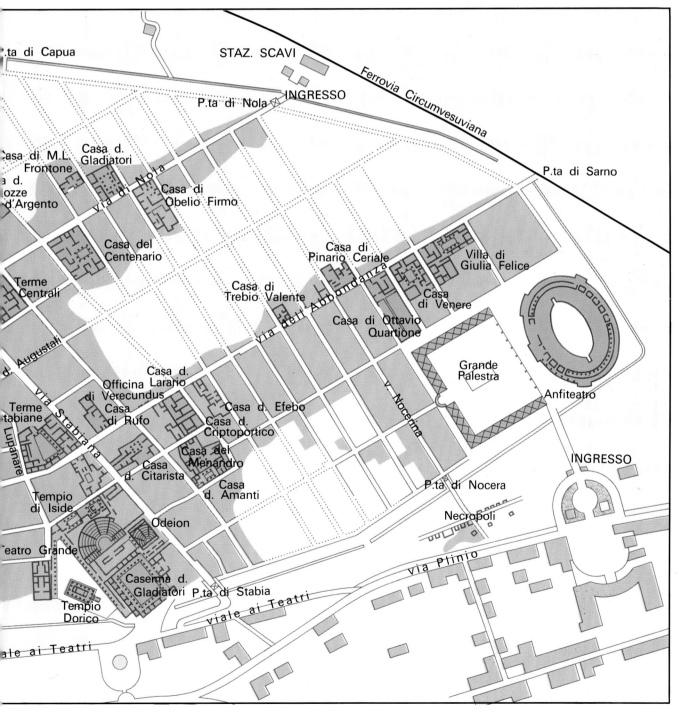

P.ta di Capua

STAZ. SCAVI

Ferrovia Circumvesuviana

P.ta di Nola ⊠ INGRESSO

P.ta di Sarno

Casa di M.L. Frontone

Casa d. Gladiatori

a d. ozze d'Argento

Via di Nola

Casa di Obelio Firmo

Casa del Centenario

Casa di Pinario Ceriale

Villa di Giulia Felice

Terme Centrali

Casa di Trebio Valente

Via dell'Abbondanza

Casa di Venere

Casa di Ottavio Quartione

d. Augustali

Grande Palestra

Anfiteatro

Via Stabiana

Casa d. Lario

Officina di Verecundus

v. Nocerina

Terme tabiane

Casa di Rufo

Casa d. Efebo

INGRESSO

Lupanare

Casa d. Criptoportico

Casa d. Citarista

Casa del Menandro

Casa d. Amanti

P.ta di Nocera

Tempio di Iside

Odeion

Necropoli

Teatro Grande

via Plinio

Caserma d. Gladiatori P.ta di Stabia

viale ai Teatri

Tempio Dorico

ale ai Teatri

The excavations are entered by way of the 1st century A.D. **Porta Marina**. Consisting of two *opus incertum* vaulted openings, one for mounted traffic and one for pedestrians, it was considered one of Pompeii's minor city gates in Antiquity since the road leading up to it was too steep for carts and wagons.

Not far from the entrance is a late 1st century B.C. building, the so-called **Villa Imperiale**, whose great portico extends along the city walls. Notable fresco decoration comprising three sizable panels adorns the triclinium. Their subjects are mythological: *Theseus subduing the Minotaur, Ariadne abandoned by Theseus,* and *Dedalus and Icarus.*

Pompeii's **Antiquarium,** founded in 1861 and destroyed during World War II, was rebuilt in the postwar period (1948) in keeping with modern museum criteria so that visitors can gain some idea of the city's history before viewing the excavations. In the entrance hall are several sculptures originally part of Pompeian buildings. On the walls are examples of Fourth Style painting from Portico dei Triclini. A brief description of the exhibits follows. Room I: pre-Samnitic civilizations, the highlights of which are Iron Age pieces (9th-8th century B.C.) unearthed in the necropolises dotting the Sarno Valley, decorative terracottas from various temples, and pottery (*bucchero,* Attic, and Corinthian ceramic fragments excavated in the area of the Temple of Apollo. Room II: The main exhibit is a sculpted tufa pediment originally part of a column-fronted temple which rose on the Sant'Abbondio Hill during the 3rd and 2nd centuries B.C. In the center is a floral

Preceding page: Porta Marina. *Top*: the houses of the insula occidentalis; *bottom*: the Villa Suburbana of Porta Marina.

The altar and fronton of the Dionysian Temple, evidence of how widespread the cult of Dionysus was in southern Italy; *below*: cast of a young victim of the eruption (Antiquarium).

motif flanked by a representation of *Dionysus-Liberus* (left) and a reclining female figure representing *Libera* (right). On the corners are figures of *Silenus with a panther* (Dionysus side) and *Erotes holding a fan* (Libera side).

In front of the facade stands the tufa altar which was excavated opposite the temple. It has an Osci inscription bearing the name of the man who commissioned it, Maras Atiniis, a magistrate, and explaining that it was financed by fines he had levied. On either side of the exhibition hall are 3rd-2nd century

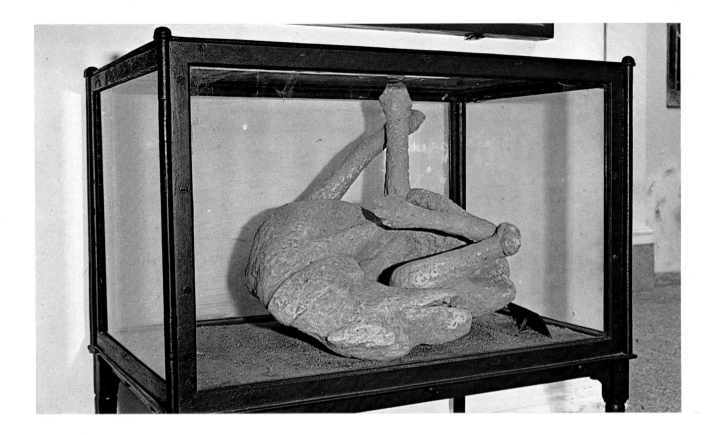

B.C. sculpted tufa capitals once part of buildings along the Via Nolana. The *statue of the Empress Livia as a priestess* was unearthed in the Villa of the Mysteries. Other highlights of the room include portraits (among them one of *Marcellus*, Augustus' nephew) and two herma figures (representing *Vesonius Primus* and *C. Cornelius Rufus*). The exhibitions in Room III comprise various kinds of Pompeian household objects. The bronze basin in the center was found in the House of Menander. Room IV: The exhibits all relate to Pompeii's economic activities. Models of the Portico dei Triclini and country estate of Boscoreale are particularly informative featuring a patrician residence, a bakery, a mill, a grapepress, a wine cellar, and slaves' quarters. In addition, there are tools and instruments (including surgical equipment), carbonized foodstuffs, stoves, and lighting devices. One of the most fascinating exhibits is the group of plaster casts showing how several of the victims were caught in the eruption.

After leaving the Antiquarium, take Via Marina (where immediately on the right are the surviving fragments of a temple dedicated to Venus, the protectress of Pompeii) and continue to the Forum.

The city's political, religious, and economic center, the **Forum** stood at the intersection of its main thoroughfares. In the shape of a huge rectangle

Cast of a dog; *below*: metal fibulae, pins for clothing (Antiquarium).
Following pages: the Forum.

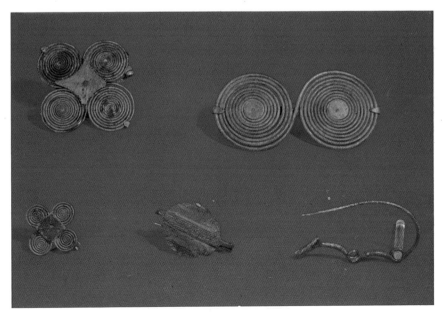

(124 × 462 feet), it was completely arcaded except for the north side which instead comprised a building, the Temple of Jupiter *(Capitolium)* and two honorary arches. The double-tier portico on the south, of Nocera tufa, dates from the Samnite period. The eastern and western arcades were adorned with travertine columns and trabeation, as part of a great renovation project started in the Julian-Claudian period (which, however, was never completed). The travertine flooring, replacing a simpler tufa version, belonged to the same project. The portico was built higher than the square (to which it was connected by two steps) in order to keep wheeled traffic out of the Forum. Aside from the bases, nothing remains of the once numerous honorary statues (actually, probably never replaced after toppling in the great earthquake). The Forum's overall plan, inspired more by Greek Hellenistic as opposed to Italic and Roman models, was both rational and attractive.

The city's most important public buildings stood around the Forum. One of the largest was the **Basilica**, a meeting-place and trading hall as well as court of justice, probably built in the late 2nd century B.C. Rectangular, it was divided into three sections by a colonnade and, according to recent archeological finds, probably covered by a single-span roof. Unlike later basilicas, its entranceway was cut into one of the shorter sides. Opposite the entrance was the *Tribunal*, the raised area on which the presiding judges were seated. It would appear that Pompeii's Basilica represents one of the earliest examples of this type of public building.

Opposite the Basilica's north side was the **Temple of Apollo**, the city's major religious building. It was dedicated to Apollo whose cult, imported from Greece, was very popular in Pompeii (as well as in the rest of

Preceding page: two views of the Basilica.
Top: an aerial view with a good picture of the Basilica, the Temple of Apollo and Forum in the center.

the Campania region) where, on the basis of archeological evidence, it was known to exist as early as the 6th century B.C. The temple was rebuilt in the 2nd century B.C. and then again in the wake of the great earthquake (although the latter pro-

ject was never completed). It stood in the center of a sacred area and was surrounded by rows of Nocera-tufa fluted columns. During the renovation campaign, the once subtle forms of the columns were weighed down with stucco decoration, their Ionic capitals painted red, yellow, and blue and turned into the more elaborate Corinthian style, while the elegant Doric architrave with metope and triglyphs overlying them was remodelled as a continuous frieze of griffon, festoon, and foliage motifs (Today however, the portico appears practically devoid

Preceding page, top: the Temple of Apollo; *bottom, from the left*: copy of the statue of Apollo, and the Ionic column that supported the clock; *top*: the Temple of Jupiter.

of the stuccowork which deteriorated in the course of the centuries.) Statues of deities originally stood before the building. Several of these were unearthed and are now on display in the Museo Archeologico Nazionale of Naples. Copies of two, an *Apollo* and a bust of *Diana*, have been set up where the originals were discovered. The actual temple, surrounded by rows of Corinthian columns, stood on a platform and was reached by a majestic stairway. It had an unusual feature: the *cella* was set back further than the *peristylium*. Stylistically, it reveals a combination of Greek and Italic influences. The marble altar on a travertine base standing in front of the entrance stairs bears a Latin inscription with the names of the four public officials responsible for its dedication. Alongside the stairway is an Ionic pillar which originally served as a support for a sundial.

Inside a niche on the Forum-side wall of the temple was the *Mensa Ponderaria*. This was a tablet bearing the official city weights and measures intended to protect the local citizenry against shortchanging by the merchants.

Continue along the west side of the portico until you reach the remains of an arcade. This was most likely the *Forum Olitorium*, i.e., the produce and grain market.

In the middle of the north side of the Forum stood the **Temple of Jupiter**. Although probably initially dedicated only to Jupiter, after 80 B.C. Juno and Minerva were also worshipped as part of a trinity. The temple thus became Pompeii's *Capitolium*, the center of the Capitoline Triad which was the very symbol of the might of Rome. When Vesuvius erupted, the 2nd century B.C. Italic-style building was in the process of being totally renovated as it had been badly damaged in the great earthquake. It rose on a tall

27

platform with a double ramp leading up to the entrance on the south side. Six great columns stood in front of it. The sizable *cella* on the interior was divided into three parts by a double tier of columns. Of the cult statues that once adorned the *cella*, only the *head of Jupiter* is extant (Museo Archeologico, Naples).

Across the way (east side of the portico) the first building in the **Macellum**, the great covered market. The center courtyard was where fish were unloaded and cleaned.

Alongide the Macellum is a sizable apsed building dating from the Imperial Age. A temple **(Temple of the Lares Publici)**, it was dedicated to the protective deities, probably in the wake of the great earthquake.

A bit further on is the **Temple of Vespasian**. The fine marble altar unearthed in the courtyard is adorned with relief scenes, among which a ritual sacrifice.

Not far from the Temple of Vespasian is a building known as the **Edifice of Eumachia**, after the priestess who commissioned it. As Eumachia was the patroness of the *Fullones* (weavers and dyers) Guild, historians believe that the building was probably a textile trade center. Inscriptions explain that it was dedicated to the *Concordia* and *Pietas Augusta* (i.e., Livia, wife of Augustus and mother of Tiberius). Unfortunately, reconstruction after the great earthquake was hardly underway when Vesuvius erupted,

The Macellum.
Opposite page, top: the Temple of Vespasian; *bottom*: the Edifice of Eumachia.

making it impossible for us to get but a vague idea of its original splendor. The structure was very impressive. Double tiers of travertine columns, each of which had a statue before it, stood in front of the great entranceway around which ran a continuous marble frieze adorned with foliage reliefs (acanthus leaves) and spirals. The inner courtyard was lined with majestic Corinthian columns. A statue, that of *Con-*

cordia Augusta, was found inside the column-flanked apse at the far side of the courtyard. Scattered bases are proof of the fact that originally the courtyard contained a considerable amount of statuary, but the statues had most likely been removed after the great earthquake for restoration and had not yet been put back. A lower-level *cryptoporticus* ran around three sides of the enclosure. It is now adorned with a copy of the fine statue of *Eumachia* which stood here (the original is preserved in the Museo Archeologico).

Crossing the Via dell'Abbondanza (which flanks the south side of Eumachia's Building), we reach the **Comitium** where the elections of the city's magistrates were held. The three elaborately-adorned buildings in the form of grandiose halls (two of which apsed) making up the south side of the Forum most likely served as the city's administrative and government center.

We shall now head down one of Pompeii's most celebrated streets, **Via dell'Abbondanza**, erroneously named after a bust unearthed along it which does not, as was first believed, represent Abundance, but is rather an allegory of the *Pax Augustae*. The archeologist who excavated it between 1910-1923, not only brought to light its original paving and supervised restoration of the buildings along it, but also managed to re-create the gardens along the way by planting the same plants that had been growing there in Antiquity.

Making a right three lanes

Above: the portal of the Edifice of Eumachia; *below*: Via dell'Abbondanza.

down into Via dei Teatri, we proceed to the so-called **Triangular Forum**, a roughly-triangular sacred area set on a volcanic formation rising out of the terrain. The forum (probably laid out in the 2nd century B.C.) was entered by way of an elegant portico of tufa Ionic columns on its shortest side. A colonnade of 95 Doric columns ran along the square, leaving only the southwest side unencumbered so that the superb view of the water could be enjoyed. Not far from the fore part of the portico stood an honorary statue of M. Claudius Marcellus, Augustus' nephew (the base of which extant). Little remains of the temple which once rose here. We do, however, know that it was built in the 6th century B.C. in the archaic Doric style with terracotta decorations on the facade and that it underwent several restorations in Antiquity. It was initially dedicated to Hercules, considered by the Pompeians to be the founder of their city, although later the goddess Minerva was also worshipped in the same building. The rectangular area laid out in front of the temple in the Roman era was probably connected to the cult of Hercules as well (as it was believed to be his burial site). To the right of the Hercules area stand three pre-Roman tufa altars. Behind them is a small round building adorned with seven Doric columns inside of which is a well. The well-house was commissioned by *Meddix* N. Trebius (*Meddix* being the supreme magistrature of pre-Roman Pompeii).

Alongside the Triangular Forum is the **Major Theater** built in the early 2nd century B.C. and extensively restored and enlarged somewhat later. Like the Greek and Hellenistic theaters, it was built into the slopes of a hillside. The *cavea* (that is, seating area) was divided into three tiers by marble bleacher seats. The stage had the classic three-door layout of the Roman theater and was adorned with niches and tabernacles. Around

the theater ran a *quadriporticus* (much of which extant) that served the same purpose as a modern-day lobby. (After the great earthquake, however, this was turned into a **Gladiators' Barracks**.)

Alongside the Major Theater

stood a tiny roofed theater, the so-called **Odeion** (or **Minor Theater**) in which concerts were held. Built between 80 and 75 B.C., it was commissioned by two public officials, C. Quinctius Valgus and Marcus Porcius.

Beyond the Major Theater *cavea* stood a Doric-arcaded building, the **Samnite Gymnasium**, where a remarkable copy of Polykletus' statue of the *Doriphorus* (now in the Museo Archeologico) came to light. Nearby was the **Temple of Isis**, built between the late 2nd-early 1st century B.C., which is evidence of the great popularity this Egyptian cult enjoyed among the Romans. Although badly damaged in the great earthquake, its reconstruction was practically complete when Vesuvius struck, so that it has

The Major Theatre.

survived in an excellent state, with its stuccowork, paintings, and statuary, as well as cult objects *in situ*.

At the intersection of Via del Tempio di Iside and Via Stabiana stood a tiny building, the **Temple of Jupiter Melichios**, in the midst of a sacred area. A Nocera-tufa altar dating from the 3rd-2nd century B.C. stands in the adjoining courtyard.

On the left along Via Stabiana is the **House of Cornelius Rufus**. A bit further on, past the Via dell'Abbondanza intersec-

tion, are Pompeii's oldest public baths, the **Thermae Stabianae**, which were first built around the 4th century B.C. and restored several times thereafter (the last time being after the great earthquake). They consisted of two sections, one for men and one for women, both of which heated by the same system. The Romans' heating system was remarkably modern: hot air was circulated underneath the flooring and in hollow spaces left between the walls. As in typical Roman baths, Pom-

peii's comprised various sections. There was a dressing room *(apodyterium)*, an indoor pool for cold-water bathing *(frigidariam)*, a warm room *(tepidarium)*, and a steam room which had one pool for hot baths and one filled with cool water. In addition, there were several other rooms adjoining the gymnasium as well as a sizable outdoor pool.

Proceeding along Via Stabiana after the intersection with Via degli Augustali is the **House of Marcus Lucretius** in the

Above: the Gladiators' Gymnasium; *right*: a telamon made of tufo; *below*: the Minor Theater.

Preceding page, top: the ruins of the Temple of Isis; *below*: a plaster cast.
Above: the apodyterium (dressing room) of the Stabian Baths; the square niches along the walls were the clothes "lockers"; the octagonal coffers in the ceiling are decorated with cupids and military motifs.

midst of a pleasant little garden adorned with a sculpted fountain. The fresco decoration is incomplete; the finest murals were detached (and are now displayed in the Museo Archeologico).

The next block is wholly occupied by the **Thermae Centrales**, i.e., public baths erected to replace buildings toppled in the great earthquake (although the eruption of Vesuvius prevented their completion). Re-served exclusively for men, they had no *frigidarium*. Instead, the was a *laconicum* which was a kind of Turkish bath and the only one of its kind in Pompeii. Various features make these comparable to Roman baths (e.g., their size, the presence of a gymnasium, and the use of building materials).

A bit after turning left into Via della Fortuna we come to the **House of the Faun**, one of Pompeii's most splendid residences. Just an average-size dwelling in its first version (Samnite era), by the 2nd century B.C. it had become a sprawling mansion elaborately embellished with stuccowork and mosaics. On the entrance is a mosaic plaque bearing the Latin word *Have* (greetings). The front section of the building has a double atrium. In the larger, which was columnless, stood the bronze statue of a *dancing faun* that gave the house its name. (The faun is now in the Museo Archeologico). Adjoining the atrium is the *tablinum* (drawing room) flanked by *triclini* once adorned with superb mosaics depicting *sea animals* and a *demon astride a panther* (both now in the Museo Archeologico). The smaller four-column atrium leads to service rooms. Next we come to the first of two multicolumned halls. The first, with 28 Nocera-tufa columns, still bears its original stucco decoration. At the far end is an *exedra* whose space is defined by means of a pair of columns covered with painted stuccowork. The most notable feature of the hall was its mosaic decoration, much of which extant. Among the subjects: a *Nile landscape* (threshold), a *lion attacking a tiger* (the lefthand of

the rooms on either side of the *exedra* which served as summer dining rooms), and a *battle-scene*. The latter, showing Alexander the Great fighting the Persian king Darius at Issus, was made from over a million and a half tiny glass glass beads known as *tesserae*. One of the masterpieces of Antique art, it is preserved in the Museo Archeologico. The second of the great halls, undeniably impressive, is adorned with 46 thirteen-foot-tall Doric columns. Proceeding, you come to the gardener's quarters, the guardhouse, and the secondary entrance from Vicolo di Mercurio.

Along Via della Fortuna is the **Temple of Fortuna Augusta** which public official Marcus Tullius built on his own property. The building rose upon a platform with a pit for the altar. Its *cella* was preceded by a pronaos with four columns in the front and three on the sides. At the far end of the *cella* was a tabernacle with a statue of *Fortuna* flanked by four niches for honorary statues.

Nearby are the **Forum Baths** which are among the city's most interesting if not largest. They bear elegant decorative motifs. The men's *calidarium* and *tepidarium* have come down in excellent state of preservation. Two halls in the men's section lead to the *apodyterium* which in turn leads to the *frigidarium* with its great round pool. The barrel vault ceiling of the *tepidarium* still bears a part of its delicate late 1st century A.D. stucco decoration. In addition, the great burner used to heat

The House of the Faun.
Facing page, top: another view of the House of the Faun; *bottom*: the Temple of Fortuna Augusta.

the room has also survived. According to an inscription, it was donated by Marcus Nigidius Vaccula. The next room, the *calidarium* heated through double-layer walls, has two pools: the *alveus* (rectangular) was used for hot baths, whereas the *labrum* (round) was filled with cold water. Around the edge of the latter is a bronze-letter inscription. It bears the name of the public official who had it set

The tepidarium (Forum Baths)

up on the spot, specifying that he spent 5240 sesterces for this purpose.

Opposite is the **House of the Tragic Poet** which, despite its small size, was filled with mosaic decoration. (Most of the mosaics, including the scene of a play rehearsal from the *tablinum* floor which gave the building its name, have been taken to the Museo Archeologico). On the floor of the narrow passageway leading to the atrium–flanked by little taverns–is the celebrated mosaic of a dog on a leash bearing the warning *Cave Canem* (beware of the dog).

The next block is wholly oc-cupied by the **House of Pansa** dating from the Samnite period, which has an unusual courtyard surrounded by an Ionic arcade with a great pool in the middle. Its last owner, as a for-rent sign informs us, was a certain Cneus Aleius Nigidius.

Leaving the city by way of Porta Ercolano, we reach one of Pompeii's several burial grounds (or **Via dei Sepolcri**). Further on is the **Villa of Diomedes** with its marvelous garden, Pompeii's largest, surrounded by an impressive portico. The entrance hall opens right on a columned courtyard. In the triangle-shaped space between the courtyard and the street is a patrician private bath. Most of the villa's decoration, including painting, is displayed in the Museo Archeologico.

A tenth of a mile down the road is the famous **Villa of the Mysteries** (which can be reached by car as well on foot), re-nowned for its remarkable fresco decoration. Built in the early 2nd century B.C., it was enlarged and renovated several times; the final version is a rectangular construction with panoramic terraces, a hanging garden, and a series of loggias. The owners altered its original patrician character after the great earthquake, adding farm buildings so that it looked more

Top, from the left: the calidarium and frigidarium in the Forum Baths; *below*: the House of Pansa (peristyle).

The Via dei Sepolcri ; *bottom, from the left*: decorated chapel tomb; *below*: a round-seat tomb.

like the home of a gentleman farmer than that of an aristocrat. The modern-day entrance is opposite the main one which, in keeping with the characteristics of typical country estates as described by such authors as Vitruvius, led right into the columned *peristylium*. The present-day entrance, on the other hand, leads to a great *exedra* with a window, making a kind of panoramic veranda. Alongside are two symmetrical terraces looking out on arcaded areas. The *exedra* leads to the *tablinum* which is superbly adorned with Third Style frescoes of Egyptian motifs and Dionysiac symbols on a black ground. The next room, the *Hall of the Great Mural*, may be reached either by way of a *cubiculum* that opens on the *tablinum* or directly from the portico. Originally an *oecus* (i.e., bed chamber), it was later turned into a *triclinium*. Its fresco decoration, dated around the mid 1st century B.C., is one of the renowned masterpieces of Antique art. Twenty-nine figures are shown in many scenes-- whose interpretation is still being discussed. The subject, according to most, revolves around the initiation rites into the Dionysiac mysteries, a cult worship that the Roman government tried to curb by issuing the edict known as *Senatus Consultum de Bacchanalibus*. In keeping with this interpretation, the scenes represent (starting from the north wall): the

A detail of the Great Mural in the Villa of the Mysteries: a youth reads the ritual to the initiate, while seated initiator looks on; on the right, a girl holds the tray of offerings.

reading of the ritual by a youth (Jachos or Dionysus?); *the sacrifice dish borne by the initiate to three women performing a sacrifice; Silenus playing a lyre, Pan playing his pipes and a female figure nursing a kid; the initiate fleeing in fear, Silenus and two boy satyrs* (one of whom drinking from a bowl that the old man in holding and the other raising a monstrous-looking theatrical mask); *the marriage of Dionysus and Ariadne; the unveiling of the phallus* (fertility symbol) *by the initiate; the flagellation of the initiate by a winged goddess; the ecstatic dance of the newly-initiated cult member; the toilette of a woman preparing for the rites* (in back of whom stands another woman, probably the lady of the house). The columnless atrium is adorned with frescoes of *Nile landscapes* beneath which were once panel paintings (now lost). The villa even had a private bath dating from the pre-Roman

From the left: a Panisc nurses a kid while an initiate flees in terror; toilette of the initiate; *below*: three women perform the ritual sacrifice while Silenus plays the lyre on the right.

period (later used as a pantry). One of the most important finds in the villa, a *statue of Livia*, is now in the Antiquarium of Pompeii.

Retracing our steps, we reenter the city and take Via di Mercurio. Along the way are the **House of the Great Fountain** and the **House of the Small Fountain**, both of which have impressive niched *nymphea* with mosaic decorations.

Proceeding down Via di Mercurio we soon reach the **House of Castor and Pollux**. Its unusual atrium is one of four in Pompeii with Corinthian columns. Most of the murals (painted by the same workshop responsible for decorating the nearby House of the Vettii) are in the Museo Archeologico. Nevertheless, some frescoes may still be seen in the rooms on either side of the *tablinum* and in the *peristylium* (the latter being a fine example of the Fourth Style).

After passing the **House of the Labyrinth**, with its double atrium and *mosaic of Theseus and the Minotaur* (room at the far side of the *peristylium*), we come to the **House of the Vettii**, whose fame derives mainly from its notable — and well preserved — fresco decoration painted after the great earthquake. The princely residence was divided into two clearly distinct ares: the owner's suite with its audience and drawing rooms grouped around the columnless atrium and the service area with the servants' quarters

Top: the oecus of the House of the Labyrinth; *bottom*: the fountain in the garden in the House of the Great Fountain. *Facing page, top*: the House of the Labyrinth; *bottom*: Via di Mercurio.

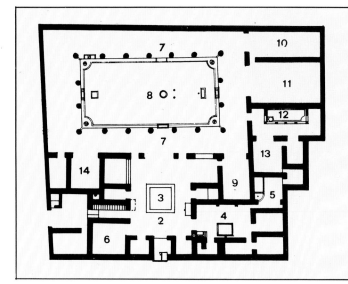

PLAN OF THE HOUSE OF THE VETTII

1 – Vestibule
2 – Atrium
3 – Impluvium
4 – Secondary atrium
5 – Kitchen
6 – Oecus of the atrium
7 – Peristylium
8 – Garden
9 – Triclinium
10 – Cubiculum
11 – Great triclinium
12 – Peristylium of the women's quarters
13 – Triclinium of the women's quarters
14 – Oecus of the peristylium

The atrium of the House of the
Vetti; a detail of the wall
decorations in the House of the
Vetti (theatrical mask and basket
containing musical instruments)
in the triclinium.

laid out around a smaller
atrium in the back. In the secondary atrium was a temple-
shaped *lararium* bearing a
painting of the *genius* of the
paterfamilias between two *lares*
(household deities). Fourth Style
paintings adorn the rooms. One
of the best known is the frieze
depicting cherubs acting out
arts and professions along the

Preceding page, from the top: a detail of the frieze of the Cupids in the great triclinium, and Cupid in a chariot drawn by dolphins, a detail of the decorations in the atrium.
Above: two-faced herma with Ariadne and Dionysus in the garden; *top, right*: the torture of Dirce; *below*: the young Hercules strangles the snakes, both frescoes are in the oecus of the peristyle (House of the Vetti).

The oecus of the peristyle (on the opposite wall note the fresco of the Torture of Pentheus); *alongside*: two details of the magnificent paintings in the great triclinium (House of the Vetti). *Opposite page*: a fresco in the oecus of the atrium depicting Ciparissus weeping for having killed Apollo's pet deer (House of the Vetti).

walls of the great *triclinium* which overlooks the *peristylium*. Beneath the frieze are panels with mythological scenes. The *peristylium* itself was adorned with statues along

the columns, basins, and fountains. The rooms on either side of the atrium opening on to the *peristylium* bore elaborate fresco cycles. In the one on the left are three scenes *(Hercules strangling a snake, the torture of Pentheus,* and *the torture of Dirce)* framed by mock architectural motifs. In the one on the right are three more mythological scenes *(Dedalus and Pasiphae, Ixion tied to the wheel,* and *Bacchus before sleeping Ariadne).*

A block away (entrance on Via del Vesuvio) is the **House of the Gilded Cupids**, once owned by the Poppea family, and in rather good condition. The entranceway, flanked by *cubicula*, leads into the atrium and siza-

The garden of the House of the Vetti seen from the great triclinium; the marks left by the roots of the plants made it possible to reconstruct the exact layout of the garden; even the lead pipes carrying water to the many fountains are in their original positions.
Opposite page: Venus fishing, in the House of the Gilded Cupids.

ble *peristylium*. All of the rooms are laid out around the *peristylium* which was extremely luminous and attractive. (Note architectural detailing such as the raised platform, and the use of sculpted marble disks, the *oscilla*, and masks hung between the columns as decorative elements). Altars to both Egyptian and Roman gods are visible (one to Isis in a corner; the other, a traditional *lara-*

Opposite: marble relief with masks set into the wall of the peristyle; *below*: the garden (House of the Gilded Cupids).

rium, on the north side). Many of the rooms once bore elaborate stucco, painting, and mosaic decoration. Third Style frescoes in one of the rooms are particularly noteworthy. Their subjects are *Thetis at Vulcan's forge, Jason and Pelias, Achilles,* and *Briseis with Patroclus.* The *gilded cupids* after which the house was named were originally part of the decoration on glass disks inside the *cubiculum* of the *lararium.*

Proceeding down Vicolo delle Nozze d'Argento, we soon come the **House of the Silver Wedding Anniversary**. (It was excavated in 1893, the twenty-fifth wedding anniversary of the reigning Italian king and queen). Built in the 2nd century B.C., it probably never underwent renovation in later periods, so that its plan is more or less typical of 2nd century architecture. The atrium is majestic with its four great Nocera-tufa Corinthian columns that rise up from the *impluvium* to support the roof. Of notable interest are several rooms adorned with Second Style paintings and a great

Right: the tetrastyle oecus with octagonal, artificial porphyry columns; *below*: the impressive atrium in the House of the Silver Wedding Anniversary.

Preceding page, top: the Quadrivio di Olconio, the intersection of Via dell'Abbondanza and Via Stabiana, two of Pompeii's main roads; note the interesting stepping stones that allowed pedestrians to cross the streets even when they were flooded by rain; even the grooves made by wagon wheels are still visible; *below*: the garden and peristyle of the House of Menander.
This page: the Thermopolium in Via dell'Abbondanza; note the store counter with containers for mixing beverages; in the background a votive lararium; a fair sum of money (683 sterces in coin), probably the day's take was found on the premises.
Below: painting in the oecus of the House of Cryptoporticus.

black-walled hall. The patrician residence also had a private bath replete with *tepidarium* and *calidarium*, as well as a swimming pool located in an adjoining garden.

Returning to Via del Vesuvio, we stop at no. 26, the **House of Lucius Cecilius Jucundus**. Several interesting finds were made here, namely, reliefs showing the Forum, the *Castellum Aquae*, and Porta Vesuvio toppling in the great earthquake; the owner's strongbox containing 154 wax tablets (found in a room above the *exedra* to the left of the *peristylium*); and a remarkably realistic portrait of Jucundus that once adorned the atrium.

Returning to Via Stabiana, we stop at no. 5, the **House of Citharist**. Its name comes from a fine bronze *statue of Apollo Citharoedus* unearthed here (now in the Museo Archeologico).

Along Vicolo Meridionale is the luxurious mansion which once belonged to Quintus Poppeus, relative of Nero's wife, Poppea Sabina, and which was named **House of Menander** after

a painting showing the Greek poet discovered inside. First built around the middle of the 3rd century B.C., it was enlarged and refurbished many times over so that little remains of its original plan. The atrium decorated with Fourth Style painting contains a temple-type *lararium*. Other frescoes adorn the room to the left. Their subjects, all relating to the story of Troy, show: *the death of Laocoön and his sons by suffocation, the encounter of Helen and Menelaus in the kingdom of Priam,* and *the arrival of the Trojan horse.* The hallway connecting atrium and *tablinum* is lined with tufa columns whose decoration consists of painted stuccowork. The so-called Green Room to the right of the *tablinum* was embellished with fine murals and a striking black and white mosaic floor with a polychrome *Nile landscape* in the middle. Even the small atrium belonging to the toilette in the right wing of the great central *peristylium* bore notable mosaic decoration. (A veritable treaure consisting of 118 pieces of silver weighing fifty pounds,

1432 sesterces in coins, and gold jewelry came to light underneath the bath during digs conducted in 1930 — evidently, the owner had taken advantage of the postearthquake renovation of his house to create a hiding-place for his valuables.) The far wall of the sizable *peristylium* with its stuccoed columns contains rectangular niches and a painted apse. In the central niche is the *portrait of Menander* (depicted seated with a scroll in his hand) after which the house was named. The great *triclinium* (entered by way of the east side of the *peristylium*) is the largest in the city (measuring 25 feet high and covering an area of over 283 square feet).

Further down Vicolo Meridionale is the secondary entrance to the **House of the Cryptoporticus**. The house is named after its huge *cryptoporticus* adorned with elaborate painted motifs.

Leaving the House of the *Cryptoporticus* from the Via dell'Abbondanza side, on the left is the so-called **Thermopolium of Asellina**. Originally a tavern, it came to light in excellent condition, with all its fittings and equipment still intact.

Opposite, in Block VII, are several interesting houses, among them the **House of Paquius Proculus** with its fine mosaics and the **House of the Ephebus** with its rich decoration, probably the home of a well-to-do merchant. Among the outstanding works adorning the latter was a bronze *statue of Ephebus*, a fine copy of a 5th century Greek original, that was

The Ephebus in the Museo Archeologico Nazionale of Naples came from the House of the Ephebus.
Facing page, top: the outdoor triclinium in the House of Trebio Valente; *bottom*: the outdoor triclinium in the House of the Ephebus.

used as an outdoor lighting fixture (now in the Museo Archeologico).

Across the street a bit further on is the **House of Trebius Valens**. The outer wall of the building was entirely scrawled with election slogans.

On the same side is the **Schola Armaturarum**, probably the headquarters of a military organization. When the building came to light, equipment was still stacked in the shelving.

On the right side of Via dell'Abbondanza is the **House of Octavius Quartio** (erroneously called the **House of Loreius Tiburtinus**). The two *cauponae* (taverns) incorporated into its ground floor are proof that in Pompeii, just as in modern-day cities, business establishments and deluxe housing often shared the same premises. Near the great entranceway were seats for callers, the so-called *clientes*, who patronized the owner for favors given and received. The *impluvium* in the middle of the rectangular atrium did not, however, serve as a rainwater collector — rather it was used as a flower pot. Crossing the small-sized *peristylium* entered from the far side of the atrium, we come out on a porticoed garden traversed by a T-shaped canal *(euripus)* bordered with statuary. At one end of the «T» was a *biclinius* for outdoor dining. Some of it is still extant, i.e., a fountain flanked by paintings by a certain Lucius. The subjects of both *(Narcissus admiring his reflection* and *Pyramus committing suicide after finding Thisbe's bloodied veil)* share a

Preceding page: the pergola and colonnade (House of Octavius Quartio).
Above: two frescoes flank the fountain. On the right Narcissus admiring his own reflection in the pool; on the left Pyramus is about to commit suicide after finding his beloved Thisbe's bloodsoaked veil. *Below*: in the garden, the tetrastyle temple from which the euripus flows (House of Octavius Quartio).

common theme: death brought on by passion. The room at the west end of the loggia (which was probably a place of worship) is adorned with fine Fourth Style paintings on a white and yellow ground.

A short distance beyond the **House of Venus** (named after a painting of the goddess in its *peristylium*) is the **Villa of Julia Felix**. The building was first excavated between 1755 and 1757, at which time it was despoiled of all its artworks, and later reexcavated in 1952-1953.

The peristyle and garden: in the background note the fresco of the nude Venus on a seashell, that gave the house its name.
This page: two details of the wall decorations of the peristyle: a fountain with birds and the god Mars portrayed as a garden statute (House of Venus).

The garden portico, supported by rectangular, fluted Corinthian columns; *right*: another view of the garden (the House of Julia Felix).

As a for-rent sign (now in the Museo Archeologico) tells us, the enterprising owner was trying to sublet part of her home (i.e., an elegant private bath, some shops, and a few apart-

Preceding pages: the Amphitheater.
Above: the Major Gymnasium

ments) — a decision probably brought on by the housing shortage resulting after the great earthquake.

In addition to Julia's private living quarters, there was also a great porticoed garden replete with a fish pond and a vaulted outdoor *triclinium* imitating a grotto in the center of the west wing.

At the end of Via dell'Abbondanza, turn into the lane leading to the **Amphitheater**, an impressive structure measuring 444 × 342 feet, which was commissioned by two magistrates, C. Quintius Valgus and M. Porcius in 80 B.C. The oldest Roman amphitheater extant (cfr. the Amphitheater of Statilius Taurus dating from 29 B.C. in

Rome), it differs from Imperial Age versions in that, lacking the subterranean level beneath the arena, its pit went below ground level.

The *cavea* was divided into three sections of 5,12, and 18 rows of seats. The top one, most likely reserved for women and children, was reached by way of an unusual separate staircase

A terrifying picture of the Orto dei Fuggiaschi (or Garden of the Runaways), with casts of some of the victims of the eruption.

and corridor. In the upper section you can still see the holes for the framework of the great *velarium* (i.e., cloth covering serving to protect the spectators from the elements).

Alongside the amphitheater was the recreational area known as the **Major Gymnasium**, a rectangular field (459 × 348 feet) enclosed within a wall. An important part of the Imperial Age complex was its sizable central swimming pool (112 × 12 feet) which featured an inclined floor so that water height ranged from a minimum of three to a maximum of nine feet.

Cut into the city walls not far from the gym is **Porta Nuceria**. Outside the city is an interesting necropolis, with examples of various types of Roman tombs ranging from simple altars to veritable mausoleums most of which date from the late 1st century B.C.

A part of the necropolis at Porta Nuceria; *left*: an aedicola tomb of a married couple (the seated statues are carved from tufo), and the remains of the Tomb of the Priestess Eumachia.
Facing page: aerial view of part of the excavactions.

HERCULANEUM

The origins of Herculaneum, the town underlying Vesuvius at a distance of only four miles from Neapolis (present-day Naples) are unknown. According to Dionysius of Halicarnassus, the city was founded by Hercules himself — and is thus of Greek origin — whereas Strabo (in this case hardly credible), recounts that it was settled by the Osci, and then conquered in turn by the Etruscans, Pelasgi, and Samnites. We do know, however, that the city, like most of Campania, belonged to the Greek sphere of influence starting from the 6th century B.C., prior to falling to the Samnites in the late 5th century. While little is known about Herculaneum's

Preceding page: Sleeping satyr; this fine bronze, Roman copy of a III century B.C. Greek original was found in the peristyle of the Villa of the Papyra during the late 18th century; it is now in the Museo Archeologico Nazionale of Naples; the villa, which has been explored using the tunnel method is still buried; it was named after the Epicurean philosophical texts written on papyrus found there along with countless artworks that now fill three rooms in the Naples museum.

Right: Theseus after he slayed the Minotaur; the fresco, originally adorned one of the apses in the Basilica of Herculaneum and is now in the Museo Archeologico of Naples.

role in the Second Samnitic War, it is certain that siding with the rebels in the Social War triggered the intervention of Roman troops commanded by one of Silla's legates, Titus Didius. Herculaneum was thus named a Roman municipium. *Its climate and setting were so delightful that, like Pompeii, it soon became a kind of resort town — even the emperor's family spent their vacations here.*

Like Pompeii too, it was canceled from the face of the earth in 79 A.D. after having been practically toppled by the earthquake of 62 A.D. Thereafter, it lay buried under an over-forty-five-foot blanket of solidified mud, volcanic ash, and debris for almost two thousand years.

While, on one hand, this solid-ification has made excavation an extremely arduous task, on the other, it has allowed materials subject to deterioration and spoiling such as wood, textiles, papyrus, foodstuffs, etc. to be preserved for almost two millennia.

Herculaneum, partially rebuilt as the present-day city of Resina, lay forgotten for centuries. The discovery of the buried city took place in the 18th century when an Austrian aristocrat, Prince D'Elboeuf, bought an estate in nearby Portici. During excavation of a well in an orchard in the vicinity, an old marble building — later identified as the Theater of Herculaneum — began coming to light. The prince decided to proceed with the excavation and dozens of statues, marble plaques, columns, inscriptions, bronzes, and the like were unearthed (many of which he carted off to the Villa Reale of Portici).

The first official excavation campaign was carried out between 1738 and 1765 under the patronage of King Carlo of Bourbon and under the joint supervision of Alcubierre and Carlo Weber (and later Francesco La Vega). The dig, an extremely difficult task from every standpoint, was conducted by means of underground tunnels and passageways. Thereafter, numerous buildings (including, temples, the Basilica, and the Villa of the Papyri) were explored, despoiled,

and then covered over. Nevertheless, the maps plotted by Weber as discoveries came to light (a practice continued by his successor, Francesco La Vega) proved of great importance for the generations of archeologists that followed.

Surprisingly, open-sky excavations conducted in the years 1828-1835 and thereafter in 1869-1875 did not produce any significant finds. Work was suspended until 1927 when the digs were reopened by Amedeo Maiuri (and indeed they are still underway at this writing). Recent finds contradict earlier claims that the eruption caused no victims in Herculaneum. Among these are numerous skeletons of people caught in the mud as, loaded down with their most precious belongings, they desperately attempted to escape toward the sea.

Only a section (that nearest the beach) has been excavated so far. Still buried are the Forum, many temples, houses, and necropolises–although how and when they will be dug out is quite a problem since much of the unexcavated city lies underneath modern-day Resina.

Top: Hercules recognizes his son Telephus nursed by a doe (this fresco from the Basilica is also in the Museo Areheologico in Naples}; *below*: the drunken Hercules marble statue in the House of the Deer.
Opposite page: aerial view of the excavations.

Plan of Herculaneum

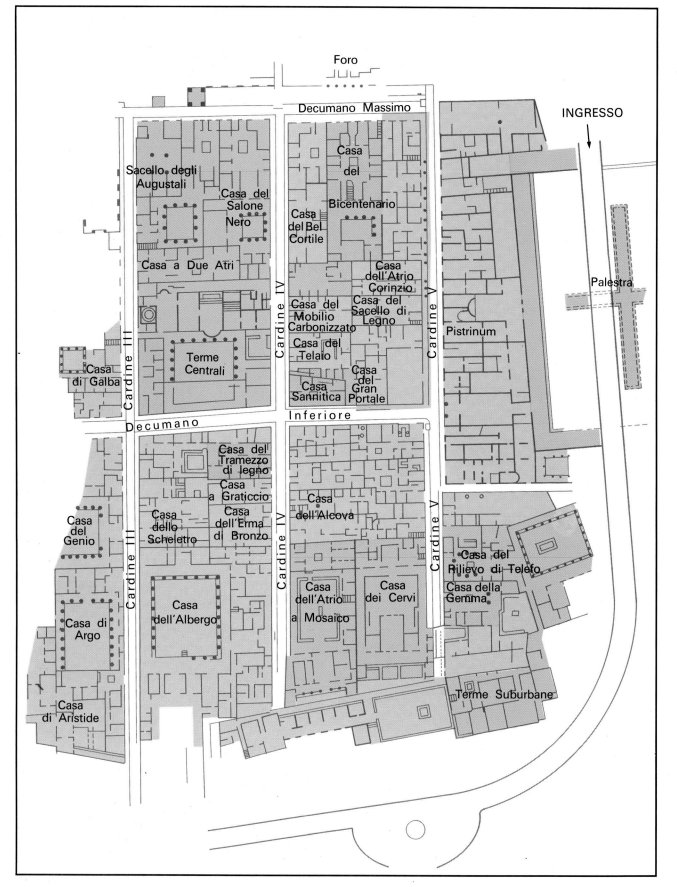

Foro

Decumano Massimo

INGRESSO

Sacello degli Augustali

Casa del Salone Nero

Casa del Bicentenario

Casa a Due Atri

Casa del Bel Cortile

Cardine IV

Casa dell'Atrio Corinzio

Casa del Mobilio Carbonizzato

Casa del Sacello di Legno

Cardine V

Pistrinum

Palestra

Casa di Galba

Cardine III

Terme Centrali

Casa del Telaio

Casa Sannitica

Casa del Gran Portale

Decumano Inferiore

Casa del Tramezzo di legno

Casa a Graticcio

Casa dell'Alcova

Cardine IV

Cardine V

Casa del Genio

Casa dello Scheletro

Casa dell'Erma di Bronzo

Casa del Rilievo di Telefo

Cardine III

Casa di Argo

Casa dell'Albergo

Casa dell'Atrio a Mosaico

Casa dei Cervi

Casa della Gemma

Casa di Aristide

Terme Suburbane

A view of Cardo III. When compared with the roads of Pompeii, there are fewer traces of traffic in Herculaneum, there are no pedestrian stepping stones, and most of the streets have colonnades (note the bases of the columns on the left sidewalk).

We shall start our tour at *Cardo III*, a strictly residential zone. The first building on the left is the **House of Aristides**. Next comes the **House of Argo**, which probably once ranked among the most splendid in the city. Its fine *peristylium*, with columns and pillars, sets off a lovely garden. The house got its name from a fresco of *Io and Argo*, now totally lost, which once adorned the great hall off the *peristylium*.

The next house the **House of the Genius**, has only been partially excavated. However, even the parts that have been un-

earthed suffice to give the impression of a splendid mansion. The house owes its name to the marble statue of a cupid that once served as ornamentation for a candlestick. In the center of the garden are remains of a rectangular basin with apses on either side.

The **House of the Skeleton** opposite got its name from the human remains which came to light when the building was first excavated in 1831. Of the original two-story building, only the ground level is extant. (The roofed atrium however, has no floor.) Once there were two *nymphea:* one overlooking the vast *triclinium* and another with an ornamental *sacellum* which provided light and air for a great apsed hall.

Retracing our steps we reach the **House of the Hotel**, set in a splendid location overlooking the sea. The name is a misnomer — even though it is of considerable dimensions, the building was definitely a private dwelling and not a hotel. However, it would seem that the owners who purchased it after the great earthquake had it remodelled into a commercial establishment comprising both shops and workshops. Built sometime during the Age of Augustus (1st century B.C.) it consists of numerous rooms radiating from the atrium, a private bath, a great *peristylium* (with a sunken garden), and a sizable *quadriporticus*–terrace built over several underlying rooms. Its poor overall condition is due not only to the onslaught of mud and debris from the eruption,

The peristyle of the House of Argo. This is one of the finest buildings discovered during the nineteenth century excavations.
The current entrance on the Cardo III was a secondary door, what was the main entrance is still buried along with part of the house. The early excavations brought to light a series of rooms on the upper floors with many interesting objects as well; unfortunately, nothing remains of these finds.

but also to the tunnels and passageways dug in the course of the early excavations.

Leaving the House of the Hotel on *Cardo IV*, we find ourselves in front of the **House of the Mosaic-Decorated Atrium** whose entrance and atrium are

Top left: A metal bowl decorated with geometric reliefs; *above*: a wooden table, pottery and other objects found in the house; *top right*: the sundial in the garden; *opposite:* the garden, the enclosed columned portico with windows; there had also been a glassed-in veranda of which onlypart of the wooden framework remains (House of the Mosaic-Decorated Atrium).

both adorned with mosaic floors. The *tablinum* is divided into three sections by two rows of pillars. The other rooms, lined up with the *tablinum*, faced the sea, allowing a superb view. A portico with a garden in the middle connects the atrium

Left: fragment of a marble oscillum from the house of the Craticum; the oscilla were decorative items, hung between columns to ward off the evil-eye; *below*: the atrium of the House of the Mosaic-Decorated Atrium; the fine black and white checkered floor, that gave the house its name buckled considerably under the pressure of the mud flow caused by the eruption.

to the *triclinium* and other reception rooms. On the east side of the portico are four *cubicula* adorned with paintings on a red ground. The adjoining *exedra* is attractively decorated with architectural motifs and mythological scenes *(Torture of Dirce* and *Diana's Bath)*. At the end of the *triclinium* is a loggia off of which radiate two tiny pavilions that served as belvederes. Several wooden structures once belonging to the building came to light during the excavations and have been replaced in their original positions. (Among the best preserved are a cradle and a small table.)

A bit further on (lefthand side) is the **House of the Bronze Herma**, a narrow, elongated building that is a typical example of a Samnite dwelling. The herma in the *tablinum* after which the house was named is most likely a portrait of the owner; it is executed in a vigorous, albeit provincial, style. To the right of the *tablinum* is a stairway leading upstairs.

The next building, the **House of the Craticium**, is of special interest from the building technique standpoint: the use of so-called *opus craticium*. Inexpensive and speedily erected, walls made by this technique (filling a brick and wood framework with the pebble and rock mixture known as *opus incertum*) are

Right: the grand Tuscan-order atrium, the opus signinum floor is offset with white tiles; in the center is a double impluvium flanked by a marble table; the cubiculum visible in the background has a fine mosaic floor and a marble table, the base of which is a statue of the Phrygian goddess Atthis; *below:* a corner of the garden (House of the Wooden Partition).

visible both upstairs and downstairs. This is the best preserved example of a type of construction that was most likely extremely widespread throughout the lower classes (and unlike the upper class dwellings meant for more than one family). A porch surmounted by a loggia preceded the facade. The impressive entrance, instead of leading into the atrium, opens into an open-air courtyard which served to illuminate both floors. Of extraordinary interest is the upstairs where the simple household objects (e.g., wooden bed frames, a marble table, a cupboard with kitchen utensils, figurines of the Lares gods) poignantly convey a sense of Herculaneum's daily life. There was also a second apartment, reached by way of an independent staircase, which, however, was rather dark (except for the room overlooking the front containing a *triclinium* couch and the tiny *lararium*).

Across the street is the **House of the Alcove**, actually two buildings joined together; one, composed of plain-looking rooms, was probably once a country house and one, richly decorated, was an elegant mansion. The covered atrium still has its original flooring of *opus tessellatum* and *opus sectile*. It opens into a *biclinium* adorned with Fourth Style paintings and

a great *triclinium* which originally had a marble floor. A hall leads to the other rooms, lit by a tiny courtyard, one of which is the apsed alcove after which the house was named.

Next door is the **House of the**

Top: Cardo IV; on the left is the House of the Bronze Herma and the portico of the House of the Craticium; *left*: a wooden press in a textile merchant's shop at No.10 Decumanus Inferior; this fine example of ancient technology has reached us almost intact.

Fullonica (laundry) which still has the tubs used for washing and dying textiles. The simple building belonged to a family who used it as both their home and workshop.

Opposite the laundry is the **House of the Wooden Partition** which has a fine (and extremely well preserved) facade. The building, originally dating from the Samnite period, was considerably altered in the Augustan Age. In fact, around the mid 1st century A.D., what had originally been a patrician mansion was turned into an apartment house and rented out to various families who shared its service facilities. To accomplish this transformation, it was necessary to add a second floor above the atrium, and fit out several of the rooms facing the street as shops. The large Tuscan-order atrium in the center of which is an *impluvium* (rainwater collection tank), conveys an impression of great majesty. To the right of the atrium entrance is a *cubiculum* which has a geometric-patterned mosaic floor. The marble table displayed inside was originally discovered upstairs. Its base is a statue of the Oriental goddess *Atthis*. The house was named after a great wooden partition that separates the atrium from the *tablinum*, two-thirds of which has survived (i.e., one of the three two-part doors is missing). Probably such wall dividers were commonly used in Roman houses, although there are no other existing examples of such wooden structures. The objects discovered in the house — among which some dried peas — are displayed in show cases set up in the atrium and *tablinum*. Off the *tablinum* is a little garden enclosed within a portico, onto which several rooms, including the *triclinium*, face.

Proceding along the *Decumanus Inferior* we soon find ourselves before the great complex of the **Thermae Centrales**. Divided — as was common practice — into men's and women's sections, the baths were built around the turn of the 1st century, but were extensively refurbished in the following years. The entrance to the men's section, on *Cardo III*, consists of a long hall leading to the gymnasium, which was arcaded on

From top to bottom: the men's apodyterium with the barrel-vaulted stuccoed ceiling; the niche in the far wall contains a marble basin used for washing; the women's tepidarium has an elegant labyrinth-patterned mosaic floor; the men's calidarium (Thermae Centrales).

three sides, and which served not only as a recreational area but also as a meeting place and open-air lounge. Off the gymnasium is the dressing room with its barrel-vaulted ceiling, benches around three sides and shelving for clothing. A great *labrum*-shaped pool of *cipollino* marble is visible in apse extending from the end wall (whereas the tiny rectangular pool once nearby is no longer extant). The dressing room leads right into the *frigidarium* and *tepidarium*. The rather small *frigidarium* has a domed ceiling decorated with paintings of sea animals on a bluish ground that, reflected in the poolwater below, must have given bathers the impression of being inside a fish-laden sea. The *tepidarium*, heated by means of hot air beneath the floor raised over little terracotta pipes called *suspensurae*, has a fine mosaic floor depicting a triton surrounded by dolphins. A door leads to the great *calidarium*, also heated by means of the *suspensurae* system, which also has two pools, one for hot water and a *labrum* for cold water. The women's baths, albeit smaller and not as elaborately decorated, have survived in better condition. The entranceway, on *Cardo IV*, opens onto a huge room that served as a waiting room as well as vestibule. From here, crossing a

small, narrow room, we enter the *apodyterium*, similar in style to the men's, which is adorned with a mosaic floor. The subject, a triton carrying part of a ship's rudder, surrounded by a cherub, four dolphins, a polyp, and a cuttlefish, is analogous to the subject of the mosaic in the men's *tepidarium*. The women's *tepidarium* has a geometric design mosaic floor; the *calidarium*, illuminated by a skylight, is sizable. The women's section also included a boiler room (serving both sections), smaller rooms off the gymnasium, and a round-shaped room for ball games.

Returning to Cardo III, on our left is what has been excavated of *Insula* VII (block) — which is only a small part of a much larger area lying beneath a modern-day residential zone. One of the two buildings unearthed, the **House of Galba**, had a remarkable pre-Roman *peristylium*. During subsequent remodeling, the tufa Doric columns were stuccoed and a podium was inserted between the columns.

Beyond the baths is the **House of the Double Atrium** whose unusual plan was probably devised to make the best possible use of the available land. Following the first atrium whose roof was sustained by four columns is the *tablinum*, the second atrium, and lastly a room of

considerable size. The living quarters were laid out along the left wing. The two-story division of the building is reflected in the brick cornice adorning an otherwise plain facade.

The **House of the Tuscan-Order Colonnade**, a fine patrician building, was built of great tufa blocks in the Samnite period and thereafter considerably modified. Following the great earthquake, it lost its aristocratic character when two of the rooms facing the street were turned into shops. The most impressive feature of the building is its *peristylium* around which runs a majestic Tuscan order colonnade and off of which radiate the *triclinium*, several drawing rooms, and the owner's living quarters. Third and Fourth Style paintings adorned the walls. A treasure in gold coins (1400 sesterces) came to light during the excavations — evidently, the wealthy owner had tried to conceal his savings before attempting to escape from the eruption.

A bit farther on *Cardo III* intersects with the *Decumanus Maximus*, Herculaneum's main thoroughfare. The first building we encounter in the Forum section is the so-called *Sacellum Augustalium*. Believed to be the center of the cult of the Emperor and the headquarters of the *Collegium Augustalium* (or possibly even the local *Curia*), the *Sacellum* consisted of a great hall resembling the columned atriums common in private dwellings: its roof is in fact sustained by four columns and light enters by way of a skylight. In the center of the far wall is a small room that served as the actual *Sacellum*, where rites in honor of the Emperor were performed. The walls were adorned with fine paintings, among which two panels one showing *Hercules, Juno,* and *Minerva,* and one showing *Neptune and Amphitrite.*

Across the way rose the so-called **Basilica**, initially, albeit partially, explored between 1739 and 1761 using the tunnel system. As described in the literature and shown on a contemporary plan, it consisted of a vast rectangular hall divided into three sections by rows of columns. The lateral niches of the *exedra* were frescoed with mythological personages: *Theseus and the Minotaur* and *Hercules*

Top: The garden and columned peristyle that gave the house its name; *below*: the atrium; the tablinum is visible in the background to the left (House of the Tuscan-Order Colonnade).

with Telephus. Of the extensive pictorial decoration which once covered the walls, some has been taken to the Museo Archeologico, while a great deal has unfortunately been lost. Both bronze and marble sculpture was unearthed. In addition to statues of emperors, there were two equestrian statues of a prominent Herculaneum, Proconsul Nonius Balbus, as well as portrait statues of his wife,

Top: a view of the Decumanus Maximus where it crosses Cardo V; *right*: one of the shops along the Decumanus Maximus (at no.10); the containers on the loft once held cereals.

mother, father, and daughters.

The **Forum** is crossed by the *Decumanus Maximus*, a notably wide thoroughfare (ranging from 38 to over 40 feet at its widest), which served as a pedestrian walkway. The markers on either side and the steps at the end of the *Cardines* served to keep vehicular traffic out. On the north side of the Forum's business section an unusual building complex recently came to light. Several stories high, it was preceded by a portico of columns and pilasters beneath which were a series of shops. The upper floors (at least two) contained apartments put up for rent.

Opposite, in the midst of the shops and workshops, is the

Top: a detail of the room with two of the four pillars that support the roof; *below*: a fresco of Hercules, Juno and Minerva (Sacellum Agustalium).

entrance to one of Herculaneum's luxurious mansions, the **House of the Black Hall**, which was named after the fresco decoration of candlestick motifs on a black ground adorning the great hall looking out on the *peristylium*. Several structures are well preserved, among them one of the wooden door frames and the temple-type *lararium* with wooden columns surmounted by tiny marble capitals.

The largest of the dwellings in the Forum area was the **House of the Bicentennial**, unearthed in 1938, exactly two centuries after the first excavations were undertaken in Herculaneum–and hence its name. The stately atrium featured a slanted roof and a black and white mosaic floor. The frescoes of architectual and animal motifs on the walls are fine examples of Fourth Style painting. At the far side is the *tablinum* flanked by lateral wings *(alae)*. The right wing was separated from its neighbor by means of an elaborate wooden partition: the wings might have served as a kind of safe or else as displays for the *imagines maiorum*. The *tablinum* is in excellent condition. Its decoration includes a fine mosaic flooring in *opus tessellatum*: a geometric pattern of white bordered by black, it has a central panel in *opus sectile*. The wall paintings are extremely sophisticated: the bottom register, composed of foliage designs on a black ground, is surmounted by a fresco divided into three sections by strips of decorative motifs, e.g., foliage, scrolls, masks, and vases. Above the three-panel fresco (depicting figures flanked by lateral medallion motifs) is a black-ground frieze of cherubs dressed as hunters. The rooms upstairs are proof that at some point the house lost its aristocratic character and had to be rented out as separate apartments. In one of these is a cross etched out in plaster panel, possibly the housing for a wooden cross that has been lost. Consid-

ering that two wooden doors could conceal the cross from view and that a little wooden box shaped like the altars holding the *lararia* stood under it, it would appear that this object unearthed in Herculaneum is the oldest existing Christian cult cross. As such, it is of prime importance in the history of the Christian religion, whose spread in Campania is known to date from 61 A.D. when St. Paul landed in Pozzuoli.

Proceeding along *Cardo IV*, we soon reach an unusual two-story dwelling, the **House of the Beautiful Courtyard**. It features a somewhat unusual plan; the elongated, low-ceilinged entrance hall served as both vestibule and atrium. Off it to the

right are three rustic rooms, and at the far end a charming courtyard. An external staircase, resembling, with its parapet and landing, typical examples of Italian medieval civic architecture, leads upstairs. The upstairs rooms communicate via the landing and a wood balcony protruding from the front of the house.

Alongside is the **House of the Mosaic of Neptune and Amphitrite.** It undoubtedly belonged to a wealthy tradesman whose place of business was the huge shop facing the street and communicating with the rest of the building. The shop, fitted with minute care, has survived intact, the wares still on the counter and wine pots still lined up

The courtyard of the House of the Black Hall; the peristyle columns are arranged so as not to interfere with the view of the garden.

on a shelf. The layout of the house is simple. After the atrium comes a *tablinum* followed by an outdoor *triclinium* which has a built-in marble table and mosaic decoration on the walls. At the far end was a *nympheum* with an apsed central niche flanked by two smaller, rectangular niches. The front of the *nympheum* was adorned with glass-paste mosaics. They depict foliage growing out of

vases *(cantaroi)* which extend from the niches to the architraves of the lateral niches. In the upper section are hunting scenes (deer and hounds against a bright blue ground), surmounted by foliage and fruit festoons and framed by an elegant cornice. The niche borders and ends are embellished with shell and mother-of-pearl designs; on the top of the *nympheum* and end wall of the courtyard are theatrical masks and a vigorous head of Silenus. The mosaic painting after which the house was named adorns the wall alongside the *nympheum*. It shows *Neptune and Amphi-trite* in an elaborate imaginary setting. The upstairs rooms (open to the street as the front wall collapsed during the earthquake that accompanied the eruption) still bear some of their frescoes. The refined taste of the owner of the house is revealed in the figurine of Jupiter and a tiny bronze herma of Hercules discovered in the atrium.

Smaller, although hardly less elegant, is the **House of the Carbonized Furniture**, which is at the same time extremely stately. Built in pre-Roman times (deducible from the layout of the rooms around the atrium

The outdoor triclinium; in addition to the splendid mosaics, note the theatrical masks that crown the pediment in the foreground, the table of the triclinium.
Facing page: this is the mosaic for which the house is named (House of the Mosaic of Neptune and Amphitrite).

and tiny rear court), it was totally repainted with Third and Fourth Style paintings during the Claudian period. The *tri-*

clinium, reached by way of an entrance hall, is decorated with fine Fourth Style frescoes depicting architectural motifs framing realistic representations of a rooster and a still life. Two rooms radiate from the atrium: the *tablinum* and a room with an oversize window facing into the courtyard. The courtyard is the source of light for a small room off to one side which has three windows. In the room several finds are displayed: a dining couch, a wooden table, as well as terracotta and glass pottery. The rainwater collected inside the *impluvium* of the courtyard-garden was stored in a great cistern. On the far end was a temple-type *lararium* adorned with stucco reliefs and paintings and a delightful tympanum resting on two little columns.

The nearby **House of the Loom** had a completely different feeling. It belonged to a weaver for whom it was home and workshop.

The **Samnite House**, one of the oldest in Herculaneum, was built in the late 2nd century B.C. and partially retains its original appearance. The elegant portal (preceded by a carefully-made sidewalk) comprises tufa-block columns surmounted by Corinthian capitals. It leads into an

Top: the triclinium of the House of the Carbonized Furniture with a dining room couch and table; *below*: the lararium in the garden. *Facing page*: the atrium of the Samnite House.

entrance hall containing interesting First Style decorations (i.e., painted stucco imitating marble). Of exceptional interest is the atrium with its elegant upperstory loggia of Ionic columns closed off by a stucco-lined marble tracery screen. Several objects that came to light during the digs are on display, including parts of a figurine depicting Venus and dog-shaped table legs. The fine decoration of the ground floor rooms is proof that they originally belonged to a patrician dwelling. The upstairs, on the other hand, was broken up into apartments and rendered independent by the addition of a steep wooden staircase. Also, the house was once graced with a garden (which now belongs to the adjoining House of the Great Portal).

The entrance of the **House of the Great Portal** is flanked by two brick columns, on which winged *Victories* have been carved. The overlying brick entablature is surmounted by a contour cornice. The house has an unusual plan: there was no atrium and the rooms radiated from an elongated vestibule that communicated with an open courtyard serving as a light source and as a collection point for rainwater. The rooms were adorned with fine Fourth Style paintings, among them the Dionysiac painting on the *triclinium* end wall and the architectural motifs painted on a black ground in the vestibule. (in the center of the latter, a charming scene of butterflies

An example of fine IV Style decorations in a cubiculum of the House of the Great Portal.

and birds pecking at cherries). Also belonging to the House of the Great Portal was a shop open on the street, which, since it was totally separated from the rest of the house, could be rented out.

Taking *Cardo V* south, on the right we come to the **House of Textiles**, the home and place of business of a family of textile

Top: the intersection of the Decumanus Inferior and Cardo V; *right*: the Thermopolium at the intersection.

The southern view; *left*: the garden (House of the Deer). *Facing page*: dogs attacking a deer, one of the two famous sculptural groups that gave the house its name.(House of the Deer).

dealers. Pieces of cloth were discovered in a tiny ground floor room.

The next house, ranking as one of the finest mansions unearthed todate, belongs to a group of buildings called «panoramic» since their positions were selected to afford the best

Satyr with a wineskin in the House of the Deer; this beautiful marble statue was found in the garden and now stands in an oecus next to the great triclinium.

possible views over the Gulf of Naples. Dated around the period of Nero (or perhaps Claudius), the **House of the Deer** is rationally divided into two sections: the entrance, with its atrium and *triclinium*, and the panoramic terrace, which were joined together by a great portico. The rather small-size atrium right off the entrance hall lacks both the opening *(compluvium)* and rainwater tank *(impluvium)* typical of Roman atriums. The great *triclinium* was adorned with fine paintings on a black ground and patterned floors tiled in different kinds of marble. Two celebrated marble *statues of dogs attacking deer*, excavated in the garden, are on display. In this wing is an interesting room with red-ground Fourth Style paintings and a marble *statue of a satyr with a wineskin* standing in the center. An antechamber leads to the pantry, kitchen, and a bathroom. Inside the great *quadriporticus* (which, however, lacked the traditional columns) were a garden, a sizable *triclinium*, and two drawing rooms. The corridors making up the *quadriporticus* were adorned with paintings, many of which have been detached and put on display in the Museo Archeologico. The garden was also part of the decoration: it had marble tables, sculpture, and mosaics (the massive bearded *head of Oceanus*, on the front of the portal leading from the portico to the garden, and horseback-riding cherubs on its architrave are still extant). None of the once elaborate decoration of the huge outdoor *triclinium* adjoining the garden has survived. The superb panoramic loggia had a

Right: the base of the monument to Nonus Balbus, proconsul af Herculaneum; *below*: the frigidarium of the Suburban Baths.

pergola in the middle, two little gardens *(viridarii)*, and two *cubicula* for midday naps. A fine little statue is displayed in the east *cubiculum* (subject: *Drunken Hercules*). Lying before the loggia was the *solarium*, a great open terrace.

Leaving the city walls by way of Porta Marina at the end of *Cardo V*, we head to the southernmost tip of the city, i.e., the

suburban district, where recent excavations have brought to light a sacred area of great importance. A space was left by the *sacella* for an honorary statue erected in honor of Nonius Balbus, but little remains except for the marble altar bearing the dedicatory inscription, the statue's head, and the base.

Right in this area was the main entrance to the **Suburban Baths**, consisting of a portal with columns supporting a gable. A stairway leads to a vestibule whose light source, a skylight, was sustained by four plain columns topped by round arches. In the vestibule is a striking marble *herma of Apollo* standing on a column which served as a spout for water which poured into the basin below. The vestibule provided

The calidarium, in the background the great tu b; it was swept along by the mud flow caused by the eruption until it got stuck in the small doorway. *Facing page*: the vestibule with the columned structure housing the marble herma of Apollo; the spout from which water poured into the basin is also visible (Suburban Baths).

A view of the House of the Jewel (*left*) and the House of the Telephus Relief.
Opposite page, top: the peristyle of the House of the Telephus Relief; *below*: one of the rooms in the same house, with its lovely marble floor; in the background of the adjoining room is the relief after which the house was named.

access to the various sections of the baths — all of which in excellent condition. These, however, were not divided into men's and women's sections and were probably used exclusively by males or else alternately by both sexes. A single room, most of which occupied by the pool, served as a combined *ap-*

odyterium and *frigidarium*. Between the *apodyterium-frigidarium* and the *tepidarium* was an elegant hall decorated with stuccoes and marbles with marble benches along the walls (probably a kind of waiting room). Above the decorative border of colored marbles (over white stucco), are great framed panels separated by little columns, each of which adorned with a stucco relief of a warrior. On high is a wide-band frieze on a red ground. Even the floor design is notable: it consists of little squares of black marble

alternating with white marble bands. The *tepidarium*, with its sizable pool, adjoins a *laconicum*, i.e., the tiny round room which served as a kind of Turkish bath. The *calidarium*, as was common practice, had a pool, albeit not particularly large, for hot swims and a basin filled with cold water. Beyond the *calidarium* was the boiler room serving the whole complex (*prefurnium*).

Once back on *Cardo V*, we proceed to the **House of the Jewel**, named after a piece of jewelry dating from the Clau-

dian period which came to light here. The Tuscan-order atrium, adorned with red and black paintings, was set off from the *tablinum* by a row of columns. The *tablinum* led into a *cubiculum* and a great terrace which was originally closed off by windows. The rooms overlooking the panoramic terrace are reached by way of the vestibule and hallway off the atrium. The *triclinium* still has its fine geometric-design marble flooring. A narrow hallway to the right of the entrance leads into the kitchen and a bathroom.

The adjoining building, the **House of the Telephus Relief**, was one of the most aristocratic in the south district. Its irregular plan is mainly a result of the irregularity of the plot on which it rises. The atrium, entered by way of a luminous vestibule, reveals the influence of Greek civic architecture in its three-part division and ornamentation, i.e., the use of marble *oscilla* with theatrical masks and satyr figures to adorn the spaces between the columns. The displays in the showcase comprise household objects, a fascinating necklace of amulets, and various kinds of foodstuffs. The bright red color of the walls and columns enhanced the overall decorative effect. The *tablinum* is reached from the far side of the atrium. On the left, two small doors lead to the rustic apartments, part of which is a low-ceilinged *stabulum* (stables). The rest of the house, laid out along a different axis, is on a lower level (reached by way of a ramp-corridor located off the *tablinum*). A great *peristylium* with brick columns surrounded a garden adorned with a rectangular basin. Off the

Two Neo-Attic reliefs of chariots in the atrium of the House of the Telephus Relief.

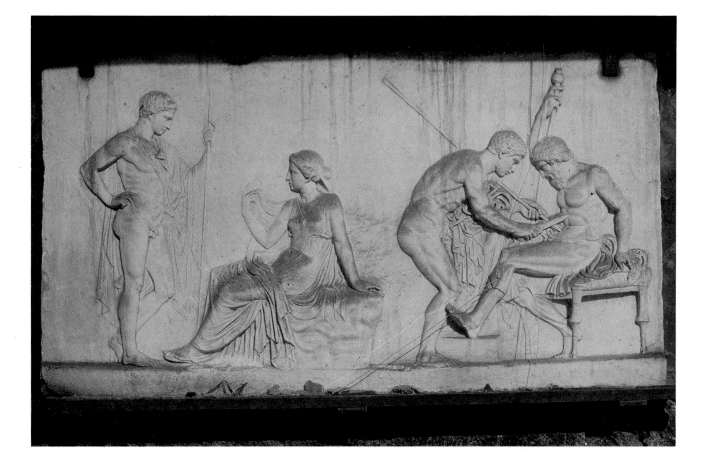

peristylium were three drawing rooms with marble ornamentation. Another corridor leads to the panoramic terrace along which are other rooms; the precious marbles used to embellish one of them made it worthy of a royal palace. The neo-Attic relief depicting an *episode from the myth of Telephus* (or Orestes) after which the house was named came to light in a room in this section.

On the other side of the *Cardo* beyond the intersection of the *Decumanus Inferior* is the **House of the Wooden Sacellum**. Despite its small size, it is a fine example of an old patrician dwelling, inside of which are

Top: The Telephus Relief; *right*: the Pistrinum on Cardo V; the millstones for grinding wheat.

fragments of First and Third Style paintings. It was named after a temple-type *sacellum* overlying a cabinet which was unearthed in the room to the right of the entrance.

The **House of the Corinthian Atrium** is preceded by a charming porch. It is characterized by an atrium with six tufa columns covererd with red and white stucco designs. In the room to the right of the entrance (paved with a geometric-design floor) various objects, including a little wooden table *(trapeza)* and a straw basket, together with its lid, are displayed. (Other finds made in the house can be seen in a showcase in the *triclinium*.)

On the other side of *Cardo V* is Insula Orientalis II, one of the numerous building projects that went up in 1st century B.C. Herculaneum. The whole block is occupied by a single building of *opus reticulatum* which runs for over 250 feet along the *Cardo V* up to the *Decumanus Maximus*. A fascinating sight is the **Pistrinum**, or bakery, in which the whole cycle of bread-making, from the milling of wheat to the baking of bread, was perfomed. In a little courtyard you can still see two stone mills (operated by donkeys whose bones were also unearthed). A stable, two bathrooms, and an elegantly-appointed apartment upstairs were also part of the bakery complex.

The east side of the block is wholly occupied by a sprawling **Gymnasium**. In the center was an open space of considerable

Preceding page: the north portico of the Gymnasium.
Opposite: the bronze fountain with the five-headed snake wound around a tree trunk; water spouted from each head into the large cross-shaped pool (Gymnasium).

dimensions which contained two pools, a large one (cross-shaped) and a smaller one. Around three of its sides ran a columned portico, while a *quadriporticus* was situated along the fourth. There were two monumental entrances to the gymnasium complex, one on *Cardo V* and the other on the *Decumanus Maximus*.

Many of the most interesting pieces (objects of everyday use as well as works of art) are displayed in the recently-opened **Antiquarium**. Among the highlights are two statues: one of the Egyptian deity *Athum* and a marble figure depicting *Eros*.

Anyone interested in getting an idea of how the early excavations were conducted (i.e., the well + tunnel system) should make a point of touring the **Theater** (entrance about a fifth of a mile from the entrance to the excavations on Corso Ercolano). The impressive theater, an elegantly decorated structure resting on a double tier of arches and pillars, could hold between 2000-2500 spectators. A distinctive feature of the decoration was the series of oversize bronze statues of Herculaneum's foremost citizens and the imperial family lined up on the top of the *cavea* wall. Also, the stage was richly adorned with precious marble inlay and columns made of African and yellow marble. Unfortunately, the theater as we see it today is completely devoid ornamentation. This is due to the zeal of its excavators, first Prince Elboeuf

The Cryptoporticus of the Gymnasium.
Facing page: some objects on display in the Antiquarium; *left*: a marble statue of Eros; *right, from the top*: a wooden bust; a brazier; a statue of the Egyptian god Athum.
Page 110: a bird's eye view of the excavations.

and later King Carlo of Bourbon, who were quick to remove every work of art, marble plaque, ornament, and decoration, from what must have been the best preserved theater to have come down from Antiquity.

INDEX